LinkedIn Secrets Revealed:

10 Secrets To Unlocking Your Complete Profile on LinkedIn.com

Patrick X. Gallagher

ISBN: **978-1492705826**

v3

ALSO BY THE AUTHOR

Publishing a Book on Amazon: 7 Steps to Publishing your #1 Book on Amazon Kindle in Minutes!

Love or Hate Email...21 Rules to Change Your - I Must Check my Email Habit. Get Back to Work and Make Money Again!

Build Your Own Living Revocable Trust: A Pocket Guide to Creating a Living Revocable Trust

Spirituality in the Workplace: A Study Guide for Business Leaders

Amazon Secrets Revealed: How To Sell More Books on Amazon.com

Trapped in a Meritocracy: Cracking the Meritocracy Code - Get Paid More for Valued Performance

"**LinkedIn Secrets Revealed**... is an outstanding book. I've read it, cover-to-cover, three times now; and, learned many hints-and-tricks each time. I wish that I had known just a fraction of this priceless information when I joined LinkedIn years ago.

Patrick and I met years ago in a brief, yet intense, teacher/student association. The (former) teacher is always very pleased when the student becomes a better teacher than he. Patrick is a master of his craft of training others to become self-teachers.

He demonstrates well his ability to assist the masses by his organized presentation, eloquent textual delivery, and instructive examples, providing many links for further self-study as the reader desires to learn and apply based upon their personal needs.

Beyond endorsement, I recommend that this book (and any probable sequels to it) should be required reading for any small business owner wanting to expand his world-wide exposure to potential clients and customers. Patrick's book demonstrates clearly how powerful LinkedIn is as a primary, basically free to launch and grow, up-front marketing tool.

Many of my clients (most of whom I have never met in person since I perform telecommuting engineering services) have found me through LinkedIn. Patrick's suggestions provide the keys to increasing the probabilities of being "linked" together even more in the future.

Patrick, keep up the fine work. On behalf of all your readers, thank you very much."

- **Thomas W. Gustin (dba GUSTECH)**
http://linkd.in/1eqnB6r

"One of the most awesome books I've read on the subject of LinkedIn. Being the most connected person on LinkedIn, I can tell you this book is right on! Anyone must read this book! Highly recommend and you will learn the secrets only few know about LinkedIn !!"

- **Steven Burda**, Amazon Reviewer: **The Most Connected Person on LinkedIn.com**

"Knowing details about how Linkedin works and what you can do to make your profile much more effective is surprisingly simple. Everyone should understand how to maximize their profile. It is your advertisement to the world about who you are and what you can do. The book provides you with the steps to complete your profile so that it will be found by recruiters looking for people like you. I would recommend this book to everyone who has a Linkedin account to maximize your visibility. Let the recruiter find you instead of hunting for your next job."

- **Bryan Murphy**, Amazon Reviewer

"Awesome LinkedIn Kindle book that details all you need to do to make your profile be found 24/7. Go check it out, save yourself $500 that some people charge to do the same things for you. I read it a few times and then put the suggestions into practice - I immediately started getting more hits (like from 2 in a months to 20 a day)and ultimately a new job. A quick read that is to the point and shares the top things you need to do to make your LinkedIn profile as effective as possible in a way that was easy to understand and implement."

- **TechGurl**, Amazon Reviewer

"Well written, precise, and to the point. Can be used time and time again while dialing in your LinkedIn profile. Quick read, jam packed with useful and informative tips and techniques. The author has done the research for you....take advantage of this."

- **Sfloores**, Amazon Reviewer

"I read through Patrick's book and it is definitely filled with useful tips...some of which was confirmed by a recruiter sharing in a seminar how to be found on LinkedIn.

Read this book and learn how to be found on LinkedIn by the recruiters searching to find candidates for positions they are seeking to fill."

- **Chris B.,** Amazon Reviewer

Patrick has been a pivotal person in my professional career. His ideas have dramatically increased my LinkedIn connections as well as my professional relationships I have been developing. He did so by recommending to make small changes to my profile and since then, I have had nothing but positive feedback. I would highly recommend introducing yourself to Patrick because he could be a great aspect to anyone's professional career.

- **Irving Hernandez**

I would like to thank and acknowledge the following people for inspiring me to write and complete this paperback book.

My immediate family - you know who you are!

And…

Ryan Deiss

Brian Tracy

Ramit Sethi

Greig Wells

This book was born and is dedicated to all my current and future Amazon Kindle e-book fans.

TABLE OF CONTENTS

INTRODUCTION

"You can have everything in life you want, if you will just help other people get what they want."

Zig Ziglar

Why I wrote this book for YOU

Congratulations for picking up this book. You have just saved yourself hundreds of dollars (or pounds). Typically LinkedIn Experts are expecting you to pay anywhere from $300 up to more than $1000 for their optimization services. However, with this book you will learn the *"LinkedIn Secrets"* that will allow you to optimize your complete profile and to become an expert yourself and <u>save</u> the **$$$$**.

The goal of this book is to give you and other LinkedIn Professionals, the knowledge and LinkedIn secrets that will help you get that call you are expecting, or your potential next job. I have carefully selected the most valuable information scattered around various places, and put them together in this book for your benefits.

What else do YOU get from this book?

The LinkedIn Secrets is about optimizing your profile so that it lands on the first page of a LinkedIn User's Search Results, plus much more. See Chapter I for a quick summary of those secrets.

In my experience, particularly in the USA, the consumer is expected to be asked to pay for stuff they do not need. You won't find that with this book. I have written and included in this book only the valuable information that you'll need to improve your profile and brand on LinkedIn.

You do not need to buy all that other stuff that some **LinkedIn Consultants** are expecting you to pay for. Plus, you have the luxury of referring to this book whenever you make the time to do so.

Be Found 24/7!

There are so many LinkedIn professionals all over the world that it's very hard for most of us to be found and seen at the "right time." It is common to experience layoffs when you're working in the corporate world. The problem is that even though the job may have gone, the person is still here.

This is where LinkedIn comes in. I believe this Social Media Platform is a fantastic way to search and find your next job whether you are already working or still searching for the next best job.

According to a blog release by LinkedIn, the social media platform has over **300,000,000 members as of April 2014** (source: LinkedIn.com - http://linkd.in/181fnAE). These members are scattered throughout the globe in over 200 territories and countries. These statistics makes LinkedIn the world's largest internet-based professional business network. If you are not on this Social Media platform – you do not have a service, product or anything to offer your customers!

Despite the fact that there are so many LinkedIn users, very few of them know how to get the best return on their investment – that is time to you all!

This is where *"LinkedIn Secrets Revealed"* comes in very handy. Essentially, you can quickly learn the steps you need to do to be found and get your next gig. Everyone has the right to work and LinkedIn helps us showcase our talents in a much better way than a letter, a resume or a curriculum vitae (c.v.) does. Your profile should be an extension of your resume, not a cut and paste of it.

In the 21st century, people are buying their products and services based on "Trust." This means they are buying based on what their friends and family are saying about a product, through referrals, and written reviews. They do not base their purchasing decisions based on what the BIG Marketing campaigns of Small, Medium to Large Corporations are advertising.

Neither do they consider who you are nor what your brand stands for.

LinkedIn Today

In today's world, if I am a potential client of yours the first place I am going to look for you on the internet is LinkedIn, then I might Google you too. I won't know your name until I have looked you up in LinkedIn using LinkedIn Search, and if your name is not in there, then you do not have a brand, service, or product to offer me.

Even if you work for a large corporate company, such as Apple, Dell, Google, Hewlett Packard, or Microsoft you still need to communicate your brand to potential clients.

That is why you need to harness the power of your network on LinkedIn - your 1st, 2nd and 3rd level connections. You should realize too that people like helping other people. People buy products based on Trust. If you have written endorsements, a photo, or a brand, then you are already established as a product or service that people can trust.

In the next 3-5 years more and more people will be turning to LinkedIn to see whom they are connected to in reference to a product or service. In the future, even corporate companies will turn to LinkedIn to use and buy some of the traditional "PeopleSoft" features they are over invested in today.

Use LinkedIn for Business Referrals

I regularly use LinkedIn to find people to do business with, even turning to LinkedIn for Nanny Referrals, A/C Repair people, Electricians and more. I never use Angie's list or any other service because of the way their **business model works***. If you come across a professional on LinkedIn and they have referrals, which you can easily check, why go elsewhere?

When you have endorsements on LinkedIn, a potential client can contact the endorser to ask about their experience in working with you. I will always send potential clients to those professional endorsements I have on my profile if they have any "doubt."

How will I find you? I do not know your name - right? Other LinkedIn users will find you using keywords and/or job titles. That is why you need a content keyword rich profile.

Learn from my mistakes and all of the books and courses I have studied and researched for several years. I offer two services and they are essentially all you need to stand out from the millions of LinkedIn users today. You can go to my website, LinkedIn Secrets: **http://bit.ly/10yWLMX**, for the latest information I have posted and the current services I offer.

Summary of what you will get in reading this book

1. You will learn the Top 5 places to focus on your LinkedIn profile, and where to put your keywords in your LinkedIn.com profile.

2. You will learn how to increase the potential of being clicked through when you show up in a search result, or anywhere else your profile headline shows up on LinkedIn platform (conversion rate).

3. You will learn to create a personal brand that will help you stand out from the LinkedIn crowd, and to give your visitors a call to action.

4. You will learn what you really need to write in the Summary section of your profile.

5. You will learn how to write actionable steps that you can follow each day to meet your SEO goals.

6. You will learn how Executive Recruiters search for potential job candidates on LinkedIn.

7. You will learn a strategy which you can use to increase your ranking and show up on the first page of the LinkedIn Search Results.

8. You will learn how to get people to ask you for a connection rather than use-up your limit of 3,000 connection requests.

9. You will learn how to make LinkedIn work for you while you focus on your clients and other important actions!

10. You will receive actionable steps to get started on your LinkedIn goals.

By the time you have read and implemented what is in this book you should be able to tick yes I did it for the goal below. Borrow this book for **FREE** if you have an Amazon Prime account. All you need is the Amazon Prime Account, plus a Kindle and you wish to read the digital version!

For more information read: http://amazon.com/prime

Get the digital version of this book below.

The USA digital version of this book is here:
http://amzn.to/12pyCNu

The Canadian digital version of this book is here:
http://amzn.to/1sKjCax

The UK digital version of this book is here:
http://amzn.to/162uYqH

The Australian digital version of this book is here:
http://bit.ly/1w2tQSk

The French digital version of this book is here:
http://amzn.to/1fd0ZqM

The German digital version of this book is here:
http://amzn.to/1eCAYQo

The Spanish digital version of this book is here:
http://amzn.to/1BGeLNm

GOAL: Increase your views per day by 10% and your search results by 20% on your LinkedIn Profile.

What's your View count today on LinkedIn? Start recording it each day, until you get to your goal.

*Example: A plumber can pay extra $$$ to get an enhanced listing for their company when someone is searching for their services (defeats organic - FREE feedback). Read more here: http://bit.ly/OcMKFU (refer back to page 14).

CHAPTER I: 10 SECRETS TO UNLOCKING YOUR COMPLETE PROFILE

"An average person with average talent, ambition and education, can outstrip the most brilliant genius in our society, if that person has clear, focused goals."

Brian Tracy

Once you learn and implement these 10 Powerful Secrets you will move well beyond the 100% complete profile position.

- **Secret #1:** Decide today what your 4-5 keywords will be. These keywords constitute those which your prospective client would search in LinkedIn.

- **Secret #2:** Create a public profile that has a vanity URL in it, not the standard LinkedIn URL.

- **Secret #3:** Place your keywords in the 5 key areas of your profile. These areas should be optimized for LinkedIn SEO.

- **Secret #4:** Choose "Other" for websites and create anchor URLs that will contain your keywords and will get indexed by Google and other search engines

- **Secret #5:** Make sure your 100% Complete Profile has a Professional Business Photo

- **Secret #6:** Connect with Super Connectors in Your Career Industry

- **Secret #7:** Request Endorsements for your profile. They also need to include your 4-5 keywords

- **Secret #8:** Include a Professional Copy Summary that states who you are, your brand and company facts. Hint: How can you help me?

- **Secret #9:** Connect with groups that have the highest number of members (bonus tip: connect with groups with sub-groups)

- **Secret #10:** Write, engage and share information with your connections via the Network Status area (hint: what LinkedIn Signal# picks up on)

#LinkedIn Signal was retired by LinkedIn.com on July 29th, 2013. For alternatives to LinkedIn Signal – type in this link in your browser: LinkedIn Signal Alternatives: http://bit.ly/LinkedIn_Signal **or use LinkedIn.com/updates**

10 Secrets To Unlocking Your Complete Profile – Expanded Information

Decide today what your 4-5 keywords will be

- See **Chapter VI** for more information on keywords

- Create a public profile that has a vanity url

- Go here for more information on vanity LinkedIn urls: Settings & Personalization - LinkedIn Learning Center

  Link: http://linkd.in/16wruOK

Place your keywords in the 5 key areas of your profile

- See **Chapter VII** for more information on keyword placement

- Choose "*Other*" for websites and create anchor URLs

- Type in this link: http://bit.ly/PnqplD for information on anchor URLs

Make sure your 100% Complete Profile has a Professional Business Photo

- See **Chapter III** for more information on getting a Professional Business Photo

- Connect with Super Connectors in Your Career Industry

- Review **Chapter V** to understand why you need a strategy and to connect with *Super Connectors*

Request Endorsements for your profile

- Go here: http://linkd.in/QWsBlz to request endorsements for Your Profile. Hint: Click on Profile, then Recommendations

Include a Professional Copy Summary that states who you are, your brand and company facts

- Contact me on at my LinkedIn Profile: http://linkd.in/PLLBUf to learn how to do this

Connect with groups that have the highest number of group members

- While you are logged into LinkedIn.com, click on Groups, then Groups Directory. Set your target goal for how many members you are looking for. Remember - the largest groups help your search ranking! Here is a link to Groups You May Like, based on your profile: http://linkd.in/13XMAYf

- Bonus: Click this link to list Groups by largest membership. With highest membership at the top - Click here : http://linkd.in/11FBGaT

Write, engage and share information with your connections via the Network Status area

- The key is - listen first! Go to LinkedIn Signal ‡ (under News) and type in one of your colleague's names, or mentor names. Read what they are saying. You can then do the same – when you are ready!

- When it comes to listening, use Linked.com/updates instead, as LinkedIn Signal‡ is no longer available

CHAPTER II: THE POWER OF BEING LINKEDIN

"Your greatest asset is your earning ability. Your greatest resource is your time."

Brian Tracy

This book is for ambitious people on LinkedIn who want to move well beyond, "I am on LinkedIn, now what!?" Short Link: http://bit.ly/RlYtgh In my book you will find numerous short cuts to getting ahead of the 300 million+ members on LinkedIn. Today there are over 300+ million registered LinkedIn members world-wide.

Very few of those registered users understand the full power of their 3 degrees of connections and being LinkedIn. This book is for you if you want to stand out from the 300 million plus registered individuals on LinkedIn. The number of users signing up online is growing by the second on LinkedIn! Are you **LinkedIn** or **LinkedOut?**

LinkedIn Secrets Is Designed For:
Members with 100% complete profiles
Members who have 250-500+ connections
Small Business Owners, Recruiters, Individuals and Entrepreneurs
Members who are 18-75 years old
Members who want to rank high in LinkedIn Search Results
Job seekers who are out of work

Note: This book is also for **LinkedIn Members** who are employed and want to maximize potential future opportunities. There are many LinkedIn Members who provide their expertise for multiple companies.

Current Stats from LinkedIn Marketing

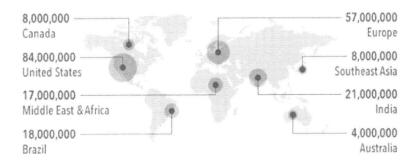

238,000,000+ LinkedIn Members

8,000,000 Canada

84,000,000 United States

17,000,000 Middle East & Africa

18,000,000 Brazil

57,000,000 Europe

8,000,000 Southeast Asia

21,000,000 India

4,000,000 Australia

Above **Info Graphic** accessed via: http://marketing.linkedin.com/audience during **September, 2013**.

As of right now (April 2014) we are up to **300 Million + Members**.

Again, my goal for you in reading this book is for you to achieve your full potential on LinkedIn. You should be able to stand out from the crowd using proven techniques that do not cost you a lot of time or money. You should also be able to use the techniques given in this book so that you'll always be employed, or potentially more employable over others!

Many people on LinkedIn have around 250-500 connections, photos, and **100% complete profiles**. Then, they get to the point where they no longer spend much time on LinkedIn. They have gone as far as they can. They begin to say things like, "LinkedIn is a waste of time!" without knowing that they need extra help to start to really move beyond what the average 300 million plus LinkedIn users do.

This book will teach you how you can be on the first page of LinkedIn Search Results within a matter of minutes. Not hours or days, but in minutes. You can do this just by learning and following these complete steps that I am going to share with you.

What do LinkedIn Members do on LinkedIn?

73%
Networking
with other
professionals

70%
Fostering their
professional
identity

2 out of 3
use LinkedIn for
business purposes such
as keeping up with
industry news.

Above **InfoGraphic** accessed via:
http://marketing.linkedin.com/audience

CHAPTER III: WHY DO I NEED A PHOTO?

"A LinkedIn Photo is worth a thousand words."

Patrick Gallagher

Okay, it's a quote that I changed slightly to apply to LinkedIn! To earn trust in a relationship, you must first demonstrate trust. To do this, you must put your true most recent photo in your profile. Having a photo that looks exactly like you during your first offline meeting will demonstrate that trust.

Your photo tells the reader of your profile that you are not a scammer, you are a real person, and you are serious about networking with other professionals on LinkedIn. You are proud of who you are.

Before I get into the details, let me start by telling you about a recent story. Let me tell you something about myself: before I tell others to consider buying a certain product or service, I first go out to find out more about that product or service, and then review my experience. With that being said here is my experience.

I recently went to get a professional headshot photo taken by a qualified photographer. The store that I went to was located in a popular Austin mall. I went in with a price in mind for a single photo. When I got there, they were busy, even though it was first thing in the morning. I spoke with a sales assistant who took down my details.

In return for sharing my personal details I asked two questions: how long is the wait and how much will it cost me?

The Answer

I got the answer for my first question straight away and it was what I was hoping for. The wait would be less than 10 minutes. I did not get a straight answer for my second question, however. Maybe the person was new, or he just wanted me to pay whatever the price for the "package" was. He told me to ask the manager who would be taking my photo.

To cut the long story short I asked the manager what was the cost? I nearly fell-off the chair I was sitting in when he told me the price. I said, "That's a lot, what do I get for that?" He told me that I would have 3 photos on a cd/dvd. He also said that they currently have a promotion that gives me 5 photos for the same price. I only wanted the one photo and I did not want a cd/dvd.

I explained this to the Manager and he said, "But we only have this package right now." He was trained by the corporate office to only offer one package. Not his fault – right!?

In response to that I said, "If you cannot give me what I need then I will go somewhere else." He replied, "Ok then, I will take a couple of pictures and you can choose the one photo, but you will have to buy the CD as I am not allowed to copy the data on to customers' USB memory keys." I said, "Okay," and it was done.

My Recommendation

My recommendation to you - hire a qualified photographer to take your photo! Use makeup if you prefer, just like in Hollywood! Just make sure you do not air brush, or use any photo editing software that totally changes who you are. Your photo should be recent. Refrain from using a photo that was taken more than 1 year ago, especially if you have changed your hairstyle etc. Remember:

Your photo is your brand!

Here are three (3) reasons why you need a high quality photo and not just any photo:

1. Your photo represents "You" as a Brand;
2. Your Photo shows up in many places on LinkedIn;
3. Your Photo is one of the most important things you need to have for a successful conversion strategy.

Again, the best advice I can give you right now, is pay for a professional photographer to take your photo and use that to upload to LinkedIn. Follow me on Twitter: http://bit.ly/Odcjqa and I will provide links from time-to-time for an exclusive deal. I have negotiated this limited time deal with a local photographer. Or you can go to my online website, if you prefer: http://bit.ly/10yWLMX

1. **LinkedIn has guidelines for photos. Read more here:**
    LinkedIn Photo FAQ: http://bit.ly/RvyrwI

2. **Think of your photo as a representative of your brand/product/service.**

    Let me give you an example of why a LinkedIn Photo is worth a thousand words. The quality of your photo tells the quality of your product or service. Example: You are searching Amazon for the next best thing and the widget has a very nice photo. But, when you received the widget it looks nothing like the photo you saw on Amazon (see photo wall for an example on page 35). How does that make you feel about Amazon and the Photo? You will surely feel cheated because the photo was a misrepresentation of the true widget. If you don't have a recent professional photo, then you are just a name, even worse you can be considered a "nobody!"

3. **Remember that your photo will be seen on various web pages:**

Your photo is visible on these LinkedIn Entities: Groups, Search results, Advance Search Results, View Profile, LinkedIn Connections, Signal*, Who looked at me last, etc. etc. As you can see, there are many places your photo will show up. Again if you do not have a photo, then you might as well not exist. If you do have a photo, make sure that it's recent and was taken by a professional photographer.

4. **Here are my recommendations on what to do and not do, in addition to the rules set in the** LinkedIn User Agreement: http://www.linkedin.com/static?key=user_agreement

   a. Background should be plain, white if possible. No photos of curtains, or anything else that might distract the viewer

   b. Your photo should be recent. Never mind if you are bald or overweight, be proud of who you represent – your brand – just like **Wayne Breitbarth** in his book, "**The Power Formula for LinkedIn Success.**" Link: http://bit.ly/OUDRMA He is proud of his age and being bald!

   c. Use maximum resolution. LinkedIn now allows you to upload a **4Mb file size photo**. So a viewer can expand your photo when clicking on it in any of the areas mentioned above in point 3. This is sometimes scary but true!

   d. Make sure that you're the only one seen in your photo, not your kids, or your pets.

   e. Don't use a photo that is more than 1 year old. Photos of graduations are great, but if you have been employed for more than 2-3 years you should use a current photo. When you meet people offline, they will be disappointed that your photo looks nothing like you today. Don't do it!

   f. I tested not having a photo (meaning your profile is 90%) complete for a month and my click through and invitations to connect went down by 10%

5. **What do people feel about having or not having a photo in LinkedIn?**

Since LinkedIn is for business people, it is easy to assume that people will think the worst when they see a LinkedIn profile with no photo in it. See a recent tweet when I searched for LinkedIn Photo – Search Twitter Short Link: http://bit.ly/PCY7Sn (Note: No need to have a Twitter account using this url!)

Example Twitter Tweet about "No Photo."

Kendra
Just got a #LinkedIn invite from someone w no **photo**, title "Looking 4 Employment", no customized invite note, no mutual connections. #delete

Which key on the keyboard do you think they will press, judging by the above Tweet and #hashtag?

6. A recent article suggests that **looks** are the Most Important Thing on LinkedIn Profile.

See: Business Insider Link - **This Heatmap Proves That Looks Are The Most Important Thing On Your LinkedIn Profile:** http://read.bi/QVffpy

7. What does The Official LinkedIn Blog say? See here: http://blog.linkedin.com/2011/11/18/linkedin-drdrew/

8. When you search for the right person in terms of services, key skills, a list of LinkedIn members show up on the first page. If one of these has no photo while the rest have, which profile are you going to view? The chances are it is the one with the best photo and the highest ranking – right?

Here are some examples of photos that do work and <u>do not work</u>.

Good Photos that do work

 Roy

 Bharat

 Frida

 Lori

 Tina

Definitely No to these photos....these do NOT work!

Bittoo

Who are you? Why do you not have a photo?

Tony

"I work v
dramatic
get more
Augusta, Ge

Current

The face on this photo is too far away and the photo shows
more than the head – its shows the neck, shoulders and
furniture!

Photo Requirements Summary:

1. Size: 4MB limit

2. What: Mainly face, but head and some neck and shoulders are good

3. Background: Plain, preferably white

4. Other: Remember to Smile - it really helps humanize you!

5. Crop: When you use the LinkedIn Crop tool, make sure you don't cut the top of your head off

6. Logos: No Logos, or added signatures (some people add to prevent copying)

7. You can upload JPG, GIF or PNG files

8. Pixel Size: 80 x 80 minimum and 500 x 500 minimum

Note: You can prevent **Google**, **Bing**, **Yahoo** from indexing your LinkedIn Photo by telling LinkedIn to not share it publically.

Why Your Photo is your Brand

Imagine you are buying a product from Amazon. You wanted to buy a Teddy bear for a loved one, a friend, or your child. You decided to use Amazon's search tool to find the right Teddy bear. You entered the keywords which give you the best search results. After doing so, the following images showed up on the Amazon search page (**Teddy Bears**).

Chances are you will click on the one that has the best looking photo, or you will buy based on the photo and the written reviews.

You need to do everything you can to entice the LinkedIn Searcher to click on your profile. Get a professional photo today. Go to my LinkedIn website for a list of professional photographers that are interested in making you look great. Connect with me via my LinkedIn Profile: http://linkd.in/PLLBUf to gain access to this list..

Example: Amazon Viewed photo online of the Product - Teddy Bear

Search result no. 1   **Search result no. 2**

Which of the above Teddy Bears would you buy based on the photos? Chances are you'll pick the one on the left.

Now, imagine what you will feel if you network with someone who is on LinkedIn and you decided to meet them in person. But before you go and meet them, you checked out their profile photo in LinkedIn. Then, when you meet him face-to-face the person does not look anything like the photo you saw on LinkedIn. What would you say? Would you trust the person?

Would you be willing to do business with them? Probably, NOT - right?

Don't leave any chances to build a lasting relationship. Make sure that your photo is professional and it shows your real face in it. Be proud of yourself! Be like Wayne Breitbarth: http://amzn.to/10rXzYx, he is proud of his photo – he is proud of his baldness and age! You should be proud too!

Remember that your photo appears in various places. Here's a review of the LinkedIn web pages where your photo appears: LinkedIn Profile; LinkedIn Connections; Linked Groups; Linked Search, LinkedIn Signal, LinkedIn Messages, LinkedIn People (People You May Know) and several other places. You may even want to add copyright "meta tags." More Info. about copyright procedures for photo can be found here: http://bit.ly/18FzsIW

How to replace the standard photo on LinkedIn

Go from this to this in  seconds.

Step-by-Step Guide to replacing your standard photo

1. Get a Business Professional Photo taken - if you need help finding a photographer, contact me at my LinkedIn page: My LinkedIn Profile: http://linkd.in/PLLBUf

2. From your CD or Memory key, copy the photo you have chosen to upload to your Desktop, or other convenient folder;

3. Login to your Profile on LinkedIn.com;

4. Click on "Profile" and choose "Edit;"

5. At the top left hand side of your photo there will be an "Edit Photo" with paper clip icon. Click on the edit photo link;

6. Click on "Browse." Point and click to the file where you have copied the photo in your desktop, as in point 2;

7. Click on "Upload;"

8. Depending on the file size of your photo and your network connection speed it may take a little while for the photo to upload;

9. Use the dotted yellow line to indicate what part of the photo you want;

10. Use the crop alignment square below to ensure your headshot fits perfectly in the window! You will see something like below.

11. Make sure you align the headshot photo equally in all four corners of the dotted yellow line. Click "Save" when done;

12. When you click save, the photo which you've just uploaded will appear on your profile. Your network will see a status update that says, "Your Name has a new profile photo." Note: This message is relayed to your network regardless of what settings you have disabled or enabled in your profile. You can delete the status update if you prefer to remove it later.

That's it, you are now done.

Examples of photos on LinkedIn wall: some are good, some are bad.

Photos courtesy of LinkedIn Year in Review:
http://lnkd.in/yir

Trivia Question:

How many of these photos do you think will pass as "professional quality business photos?"

The answer is:

Roughly fourteen (14) are professional business photos.

Ask a Professional Photographer and they will be glad to tell you which ones would get left on the cutting-room floor!

CHAPTER IV: SEARCH LIKE A RECRUITER OR HEADHUNTER – BE FOUND!

"No one lives long enough to learn everything they need to learn starting from scratch. To be successful, we absolutely, positively have to find people who have already paid the price to learn the things that we need to learn to achieve our goals."

Brian Tracy

You are going to be using "Advanced Search," a lot. You should learn how to use it now, so that you'll understand how others are searching for you too!

Here is a quick link to it: LinkedIn Advance Search: http://linkd.in/1a1fuHP

The most recent LinkedIn tool bar now has a drop down list of categories you can search by. For example: People, Groups, Job etc.

How do Recruiters find you - Quite Simply they find you - FAST! Not like the old days! In the old days they had to make phone calls, or other methods.

Here is what Recruiters typically do to find you on LinkedIn.

Go to the next page and look at the advance search page to see what key fields are used to conduct recruiter searches.

1. They usually use 5-7 keywords to narrow their search results.

2. They type in a zip or postcode to find a candidate whose credentials are close to the position they are searching for – see Illustration 1.

3. They use a Job title, like Senior Program Manager.

4. They use an Industry specific filter.

5. Lastly, they use the Sort by connections to ensure they have the most connected people showing up in their search results (this is an extremely important step).

Note: **Point 5** is no longer an option, since early 2013. This feature was something I used daily and sadly miss. I use LinkedIn Updates now.

Illustration 1

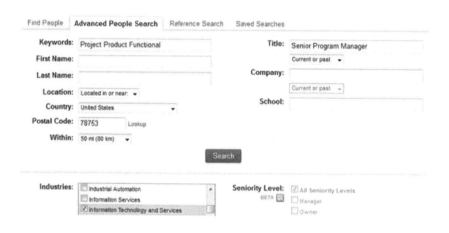

In the above example I have used keywords: **Project, Product**, and **Functional** with a title of: **Senior Program Manager**. I have also filtered the search with a local zip code. In this case the zip used was **78753**. The image on the next page shows the keyword search results.

Information Technology and Services ○

164 results

Sort by: Relevance ▾ V

Terry (2nd)
Sr. Director, **Project** Management Office at
Texas Area · Information Technology and Services
498 connections · 19 recommendations

Connect

Current: Sr. Director, **Project** Management ... more
Past: **Project Manager / Cross Functional** ... more
Groups: Role1's CEO/CXO Network · Seilevel - ... more
▸ 3 shared connections · Similar

Ram (2nd)
Senior IT Program Manager
· Information Technology and Services
500+ connections · 15 recommendations

Connect

Current: Adjunct Professor & Best Practices ... more
Past: **IT Program Manager**, Solution at ... more
Groups: Master Data Management Interest ... more
▸ 2 shared connections · Similar

Donna (2nd)
Experienced IT Professional
Texas Area · Information Technology and Services
360 connections · 2 recommendations

Connect

43

These were the top 3 candidates, sorted by relevance. The screen shots below shows what happens when I change the filter to view by connections.

Results above show the search results when sorted by connections. When you get the hang of using advanced search, you will get the first page to only show 1 page of results! Then you will see how powerful this *LinkedIn Secrets Revealed* book is!

Tip: By following the above steps you can find out for yourself if someone has more connections than you. Do this test for a particular job title and industry. In this example below, **Brad** has more connections than **Ram** and **Tony**. You can use this kind of search technique to see if someone has a higher number of LinkedIn connections than you.

This is most useful when you reach the 500+ connection milestone. You will get the 500+ connection badge too!

When I add the keywords: **PM** and **IT** to the keywords filter box I get the 164 results reduced to 48 results. Add another key word, or expand your job title and the results will reduce even more.

How do Recruiters search for their next best candidate?

When recruiters are running out of time and they need a short list of interview candidates, this is what they will type in to "Advanced Search" on LinkedIn. See screen shots below.

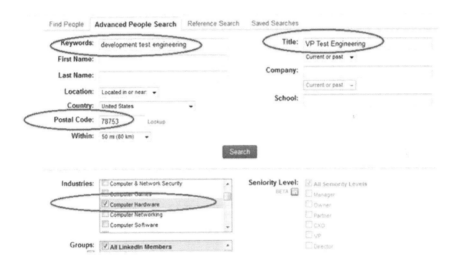

The above advanced search settings only bring up 3 profiles in the search results page. That is the power of keyword searches on LinkedIn. You want to be on that first page. That is why you need to know what keywords people are searching for on LinkedIn.

Action Steps

1. List the keywords that you think recruiters would use to search for you;

2. Enter your zip or postal code;

3. View the results - where do you show up today?

4. Record the results, make the changes and then record the new results

CHAPTER V: WHAT'S YOUR CONNECTION STRATEGY?

"The fact is that no one is better than you are and no one is smarter than you are. If they are doing better, it is largely because they have developed their natural talents and abilities more than you have."

Brian Tracy

Offline networking typically works well when you have a plan before you meet. You will also need to be thinking about the other person's needs more than your own. In order to improve your network connections on LinkedIn, you must decide today what your goal is and how you will implement it. For example, it might be to double your connections within 12 months.

So go from say, 500 connections to 1000 connections. Keep in mind too of the LinkedIn limitations and pitfalls. You can only request **3000 connections** within the life of your LinkedIn profile. You also have 5 IDK strikes and then you are out. On LinkedIn when you are on the *"Connect"* screen, as shown below, you will be reminded of this IDK issue.

See next page screenshot…

Invite Ivor to connect on LinkedIn

How do you know Ivor?

- ○ Colleague
- ○ Classmate
- ○ We've done business together
- ● Friend
- ○ Groups
- ○ Other
- ○ I don't know Ivor

Include a personal note: (optional)

> I'd like to add you to my professional network on LinkedIn.
>
> - Patrick

Important: Only invite people you know well and who know you. Find out why.

Send Invitation   or Cancel

Circled above you also do not want to get the dreaded IDK response from the potential connection. Be smart!

A Connection Strategy: **Connect with Super Connectors**

Trivia Question:

Who or what are Super Connectors?

The Answer is:

Super Connector are LinkedIn Members who are very well connected on LinkedIn. Super Connectors typically have >1000+ connections. Some are now saying >5000 connections.

One connection secret you could consider using is connecting with a "Super Connector."

I have listed steps to the connection strategy on the next page.

Super Connector – Connection Strategy Action Steps

1. Use the Keywords that you came up with in Chapter IV;

2. Go to "Advanced Search;"

3. Type in the 5 keywords;

4. Enter your zip code with a short radius for your zip;

5. Scroll to the bottom of the screen and select search by connections; (sadly with latest LinkedIn roll-out, as from February, 2013 this feature has been disabled)

In the search results, send connection requests to the **first 5 LinkedIn members that appear on the first page**. Try to connect with people that have the words "*open networker*" or "*LION*" somewhere on their profile. If you cannot sort by connections, just pick the members that have **500 connection**s. Basic (Free) accounts can only view the first 100 results. The screen shot below shows the Group Logo for TopLinked.com and will usually appear at the end of the LinkedIn Member's Profile.

If you do not want to connect with people you haven't met before, then you can easily fix that by sending them a connection request asking them to meet offline. The best way to do this is to join the group where they are a member of first, then you can connect to them through your group connection (Hint: This is a **BIG Secret Tip**).

Action Steps

1. Follow the steps outlined above in the Super Connector action steps;

2. Click on the first profile at the top of the page. Select a group where the person belongs to and see if you are already a member of that group. If not, join the group;

3. Then email them directly.

Member

As you can see from the screen shot above the super connector is already a member (shown in a grey box, as above) of the same group as the person performing the search.

If you had the same result, then all you have to do is go to the group, click members, and then send a message. It's just that easy!

Note: Groups on LinkedIn.com got a refresh recently, so you no longer see the green highlight you saw before.

CHAPTER VI: WHAT ARE YOUR KEYWORDS?

"The key to success is to focus our conscious mind on things we desire not things we fear."

Brian Tracy

You have a job right? Let's say you are an **IT Project Manager**. You could search for jobs in your area with those three key words and pick one job profile.

Let's review an example.

- Step 1: Go to indeed.com;

- Step 2: Type in the words, "**IT Project Manager**" as shown below:

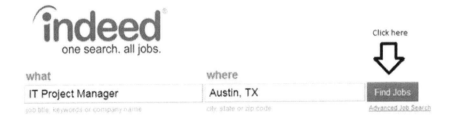

- Step 3: Review the results;

- Step 4: Click on the link as below and review the search results;

- Step 5: Copy and paste the job description into a text file;

- Include everything relevant to the position. Include: Responsibilities, Qualifications, Minimum Requirements, Work Experience, Education, Special Skills, Certifications, etc.

- Step 6: Go to **wordle.net** and paste your text from your text file into the web application;

Wordle™   Home   Create   Gallery   Credits   News

Wordle is a toy for generating "word clouds" from text that you provide. The clouds give greater prominence to words that appear more frequently in the source text. You can tweak your clouds with different fonts, layouts, and color schemes. The images you create with Wordle are yours to use however you like. You can print them out, or save them to the Wordle gallery to share with your friends.

- Step 7: Review the "Word cloud," for the job description you copied into wordle.net. The Word cloud should look like the one you see below

- Step 8: Look for the largest words; these words are going to be your keywords. So for this example I would list 5 keywords max.

- Step 9: Create your keyword file similar to the one shown below and record your keywords. You will need these later.

	A	B
1	Number	Keyword
2	1	Project
3	2	Development
4	3	Software
5	4	Design
6	5	Requirements

The above table illustrates your keywords you will use for your profile.

You will see from my list, a couple of things. 1) I picked the largest word and 2) I did not include words that LinkedIn Members/Recruiters are most likely not going to search for.

Example: **Skills**. This won't be one of your keywords ☺!

Go to the Bonus Section and review my *Game Changer Tool* that I use to find out what are the highest ranked keywords on Google™, before sprinkling the keyword throughout my profile.

CHAPTER VII: WHERE DO I PUT THESE KEYWORDS IN MY LINKEDIN PROFILE?

"There is one quality which one must possess to win, and that is definiteness of purpose, the knowledge of what one wants, and a burning desire to possess it."

Napoleon Hill

According to current research the best places to put these keywords in your profile are:

#1 Headline (aka Tagline)

#2 Summary

#3 Position #1 - current job;

#4 Position #2 - previous job;

#5 Specialties

On the next few pages of this book you will see an example of a **LinkedIn profile** with appropriate keyword placement. You have to put your keywords into your profile similar to the examples below so that you'll end up in the first page of the search results. I have circled the sections in the LinkedIn Profile of Stacy where you would have to put your own keywords.

Stacy Donovan

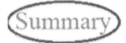

Most Connected Woman on LinkedIn # Social R

link2stacy@

Summary

Most Connected Woman on LinkedIn
LION # TopLinked # Accept All # No IDK

Note: Stacy Donovan will have changed her headline and summary several times, since this one was captured for this book.

Specialties Profile Section

Expertise in Social Networking / Social Media Recruiting (via LinkedIn, Twitte
Google+, etc.). Training, consulting and coaching on cutting-edge social media
techniques.

Experience Profile Section

Experience

Digital Recruiting Consultant / Trainer / Speaker   Position #1
Stacy
July 2011 - Present (1 year 2 months)   San Diego

I provide digital recruiting / social media recruiting consulting services to HR / Recruiting clients
including group training camps, onsite sessions, webinars and on a one-on-one basis, teaching
Recruiters how to leverage social media (LinkedIn, Twitter, Facebook, Google+, etc.) to source
/ hire passive candidates, develop a strong employment brand, improve candidate experience,
increase employee referrals, streamline recruiting efforts, cut advertising costs, decrease time
to fill and develop an employment brand to market the company as an employer of choice.

For additional information, please visit my site at

Stacy   has 1 recommendation (1 partner) including:
(2nd) David   Group Leader, Utility Discount Warehouse Club
Recommend Stacy Donovan work at Stacy Donovan Zapar Consulting

Blogger   Position #2
Stacy
2010 - Present (2 years)

Blogging about LinkedIn, networking, job search and recruiting tips and tricks since 2010.
100,000+ page views and featured on 50+ other sites, including The Huffington Post, The
Examiner, YouTern, BlogHer, Scoop.it, Smashfly Technologies, ResumeBear, Career CoPilot
and many others. For the full list, please visit: http://www.   om/p/media.html
Recommend Stacy: work at Stacy Zapar's Blog - \

That covers where you put all your keywords. You may also opt to put some of the keywords in Sections #3 and #4 (refer back to Position #1 etc.), but the ones in this example are more crucial. If this seems like a lot of work I can help you make these updates for you. For further information you can contact me at my LinkedIn Profile: http://linkd.in/PLLBUf

Just for reference the person's profile that appears with the most connections (using the keywords in this example) in Austin today is as on the next page*. A recruiter will probably contact the first three people that appear at the top of the advanced search results. The Key is to get to the top, or at least, on the first page of the search results.

*Note: Keep in mind that this can change every minute, hour, or day on LinkedIn.com.

Example Search Result using the keywords in the table

179 results

Charley (2nd)
IT Director | Senior **IT Project Manager** | PMP | Open to Advancement Opportunities
Austin, Texas Area · Information Technology and Services
500+ connections · 17 recommendations

Current: Founder | Executive Director at .... more
Past: Senior **IT Project Manager** | PMP at ... more
Groups: Executive Suite · TopLinked Executives... more
▸ 63 shared connections · Similar

Gaurav (PMP, MBA) (2nd)
MBA Student at McCombs School of Business, University of Texas at Austin
Austin, Texas Area · Financial Services
500+ connections

Current: MBA Student at McCombs School of ... more
Past: **Project / Program Manager** at AMD, ... more
Groups: Coaches Exchange · NUS · Banking Connects... more
▸ 38 shared connections · Similar

Jim Bob (2nd)
SharePoint Front-end Developer, Speaker, Author, Connector, and Community Organizer. What can I do for you?
Austin, Texas Area · Information Technology and Services
500+ connections · 53 recommendations

This is the new **Advanced search** tool popup that was introduced by LinkedIn.com in **2013**.

On the next page you will see where the keywords show up on Charley's profile. It is very useful as it gives you a <u>hint</u> to where your keywords should be placed too!

Charley

**IT Director | Senior IT Project Manager |
PMP | Open to Advancement Opportunities**

Austin, Texas Area | Information Technology and Services

Current   ACS, a Xerox Company, Leaders in Technology
in the Greater Austin Area

Previous   Avery Dennison, Time Warner Cable, Wachovia
Bank

Education   Engineering at The University of Texas at Austin

Note: I have circled where the keywords get highlighted by LinkedIn.com when you click on someone that appears in the search results using your <u>unique</u> keywords.

Senior Project Manager
Glaxo Smith Kline GSK
2003 – 2004 (1 year)

Senior Project Manager
Analysts International
Public Company; 501-1000 employees; ANLY; Information Technology and Services in
2002 – 2004 (2 years)

Senior Project Manager
Capital One
Public Company; 10,001+ employees; COF; Financial Services industry
2002 – 2003 (1 year)

Charley has 1 recommendation (1 client) including:
(2nd) Pratap Pandey

Senior Project Manager
Winstar Communications - Professional Services Division
Public Company; 1001-5000 employees; WCII; Telecommunications industry
2000 – 2001 (1 year)

Charley has 1 recommendation (1 manager) including:
(2nd) Scott Pobolsky, Director, Winstar

Senior Project Manager

As you can see the **Project Manager** title appears in many locations for this LinkedIn Profile. Hence it appears <u>high</u> in the search results.

Question: What words are not considered keywords? Checkout **Ms. Donna Serdula,** [Link: http://bit.ly/UhfUTP] for her opinion on this.

What's your conversion Strategy?

When you have a keyword loaded profile your search metrics will go up. For example, you might see, "**You have shown up in search results 67 times in the past 3 days.**" However the "**Your Profile has been viewed by 7 people in the past 3 days**" will indicate that you need a <u>View conversion strategy</u> for converting the clicks from the searches you are getting to views.

You need to get your viewed number up to at least half of your search results. A small goal would be to get at least 1 view per day.

Example:

Who's Viewed Your Profile?

7 Your profile has been viewed by 7 people in the past 3 days.

67 You have shown up in search results 67 times in the past 3 days.

Now that you have your profile loaded with keywords, how do you ensure that the recruiter clicks on your profile?

Action Steps

1. Make sure you have an inviting, pleasing headline.

2. Get a great professional photo.

3. Create a Persuasive summary section [sales copy*****].

Use Smart techniques to measure your conversion rate. You can click on "Who has viewed my profile," but you will need to use a paid account to see all of the people that have clicked on your profile. The basic account only lets you see a limited amount. It might be worth a trial signup if you are currently looking for a job. As a thank you to you for buying this book, here is a <u>**secret**</u> link that will get you the **Premium account** for least amount of money: http://linkd.in/18e2fCq [referred to as **LinkedIn Premium Plus**].

Within your LinkedIn website links you can link to your personal website and then make the link traccable. You can count how many people have gone from LinkedIn to your personal website. Use Google Analytics for that information.

Here is a recent **Career Trends newsletter** I contributed to. With the help of other LinkedIn Experts (Wayne Breitbarth: http://linkd.in/18irMfG & Melonie Dodaro: http://linkd.in/18KHjH1). We discuss the **LinkedIn Dos and Don'ts**: - http://bit.ly/Ywqbym

---

* Sales Copy: Is a Call to Action for your products or services. Example: You could put your phone number in your summary section and say, "Call me on this number now!"

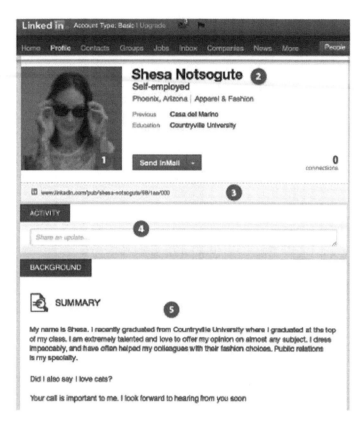

The screen shot is from "**LinkedIn Dos and Don'ts – Career Newsletter.**" **Link:** http://bit.ly/Ywqbym

CHAPTER VIII: LINKEDIN GOALS –
WHAT DO I DO NEXT?

"Goals should be written in the following format. They should use the 3 P's. This means they should be a) Positive, b) Written in the Present tense and c) Personal."

Patrick Gallagher

Future Goal:

Example: I have 10,000 LinkedIn Connections.

Using "**I**" is the Personal Pronoun.

Using "**have**" means you already have the connections.

Positive: Means you have not included the words "do not" which is the negative.

Example: "I do not smoke," would be a negative goal.

On the next page you will find a list of **10 goals** which could move you beyond the 100% complete profile. Typically LinkedIn Members complete their profile and then stop making any further updates, or sending out network status updates.

10 LinkedIn Goals to Execute Right Now!

1. Take a professional business photo and upload the photo to LinkedIn. Contact me through my LinkedIn Profile if you need assistance with that. I have several photographers in my network -My LinkedIn Profile: http://linkd.in/PLLBUf

2. Create your relevant **5-7 LinkedIn keywords**.

3. Update your profile with the keywords in the 5 key areas. Refer to **Chapter VII: Where do I put these keywords in my LinkedIn Profile?**

4. Write down on a piece of paper one goal, indicating how many connections you want to get after a certain time frame. For example, write: "**I have 1000 online LinkedIn Network Connections.**" Make it time bound, by adding a date.

5. Start listening to your LinkedIn network connections - use LinkedIn Signal (Linkedin.com/signal), or go to your LinkedIn home page, then news, and then Signal (**removed on 7/29/13**).

6. Engage with your connections; use the "Like" and "Comment" buttons on your LinkedIn home page.

7. Join the largest networked groups. These are the ones that have the **most members** in your industry, or profession. Join as many as 50 groups if you can. Even better if they have sub-groups!

8. Work more on networking with your offline connections. Whenever you meet a new person ask them if they are on LinkedIn and connect with them, if possible online too. I recommend you send the LinkedIn Connection request on the same day.

9. Create a daily action plan that includes no more than 15-30 minutes of activity on LinkedIn per day. Short of time - put aside 5 minutes a day instead!

10. Hire a LinkedIn Expert (like me) to help you improve your LinkedIn Profile - go to My Website: http://bit.ly/10yWLMX today!

One of the goals I am working on right now is increasing my **LinkedIn Profile Views by 20%.** The last chapter explains how you can formulate a strategy to achieve that goal.

For **point 9** above you can setup timed Network Status updates. You can use **Bufferapp.com** and this will help you send out regular updates over a 2 week period for FREE. Or you can use an alternative social media scheduler.

Also check out - http://www.linkedin.com/updates to see what your network is chatting about!

CHAPTER IX: CONNECT TO SUPER CONNECTORS – HOW TO GROW YOUR NETWORK

"Successful people are always looking for opportunities to help others. Unsuccessful people are always asking, What's in it for me?"

Brian Tracy

What do successful people (aka **Super Connectors**) do on LinkedIn and in offline networking situations? They connect you with other successful people. You should do the same on **LinkedIn.com**.

I love getting emails from my existing connections that request me to introduce them to other **LinkedIn Members** they wish to connect with.

With that being said I want to introduce you to a powerful way of moving your focus away from **Network Search Statistics.** Instead concentrate on ways you can increase your views from <u>average</u> to <u>Super!</u>

Let's assume you have:

1)   500 Connections
2)   Current member of 50+ Groups (I am a member of 97)

And here are the 3 Powerful steps that will help increase your Linked In Profile views per day.

a)   Get active on LinkedIn, daily – spend 10-15 minutes creating content, sharing content and liking/commenting on your LinkedIn Member Network updates. Respond to Group comments etc.

b)   Click on Profile, Who's Viewed Your Profile – return the favor and click on their profile. Send connection requests to other Super Connectors (500+ badge)

c)   Use the "**People You May Know**" feature – find it on the home page and click on See More. Send an invitation to connect with like-minded individuals and use an effective connection request

Having a **100% complete profile** with all the Bells and Whistles, an enticing, smiling business photo will impact your connection request. Here is an example of a short, but concise connection request I recently sent to a Mentor.

"**Mark, we are in the Dale Carnegie Leadership class together. We should be connected online too. I can share my large network with you. Thanks for connecting.**

Best,

Patrick."

Finally remember to connect with commonalities. (1) Similar Connections, (2) Location, (3) Skills in common and (4) Location – use your zip or postcode to find people in the Advanced Search feature of LinkedIn Search.

Lastly, in order to measure your success, keep a record of your baseline and date in a spreadsheet. You will want to keep a note of your 90 day trends, Who's Viewed Your Profile and how many times you have appeared in LinkedIn Search (similar to below).

How many times you appeared in LinkedIn Search

13,492

Note: The image on the previous page shows one week of network search statistics. This was how many time my LinkedIn Profile was showing up in LinkedIn Network Search results.

CHAPTER XI: GETTING LINKEDIN TO YOUR RESUME

"Storytelling is the most powerful way to put ideas into the world today."

Robert McKee

If you are serious about increasing your LinkedIn views and helping Google to find your resume – you need to do this. You should think about <u>Linking</u> your Resume back to your online **LinkedIn Profile**.

This requires a webserver address (url) and you will need to edit your resume so it can be uploaded to your webserver etc. Here is a summary of what you need.

Step 1

1. Microsoft Word Resume/CV saved as a web page – e.g. Patrick-Gallagher-Resume.html
2. Web Domain e.g. your-name-.com
3. Use your 4-5 keywords in the tag section as below
4. Get a GMAIL account – you will use this for Webmaster tools
5. Once you have a resume/CV that you have saved as a .html file edit the file and optimize the html. See the Optimize section

Step 2

1. Upload your Resume/CV to your web server
2. Using the Google Webtools – add the resume page [e.g. yourname.com/Resume.html to the Google Webmaster Fetch as Google
3. Google will then fetch your resume as a site to index
4. Start adding back-links to your resume page on multiple sites – see
   https://www.google.com/#q=howtoaddbacklinkstoyoursite
5. Build as many as you can leaving questions/answers on

forums , or blogs of your choice

This should help you to get around 60-100 views a month from Google.

Here is an example HTML file where I have added the tags to my resume. Make sure it is at the top of the HTML, so Google can see it.

Example html file
```
<html>

<head>
<meta       http-equiv=Content-Type       content="text/html; charset=windows-1252">
<title>Resume of Your Name keyword1 Keyword2 keyword3 Keyword4</title>
<meta  name="Keyword1  Keyword2  Keyword3  Keyword4 Keyword5"
content="resume, your company product your town.">
<meta name="Your Name as it appears on your LinkedIn Profile"
content="resume of a IT Project Program Manager with 10 years of Technology experience.">
</head>
```

Here is a link to a site that explains this META keyword in more detail: http://www.job-hunt.org/resumeHTMLmeta.shtml

My current network search results on LinkedIn are around 14,000 per week. You can increase your results too by adding back links to your LinkedIn Profile.

CHAPTER XII: OUTLOOK SOCIAL CONNECTOR

"I'm very tech-forward. However, I also think hitting the pause button is not a bad thing, and really connecting with people one-to-one viscerally, having a connection with someone, is really important."

Ashton Kutcher

Do you use Microsoft Outlook at work? If you do there is a wonderful tool that I champion. I champion it because I love several features of it that help me stay connected with my LinkedIn Members. It's the pictorial view of all your connections in one place.

If your company uses Microsoft Outlook I strongly recommend you ask if you can use it – check with your manager, IT department, as it will undoubtedly require bandwidth from the updates this Social Media network needs.

LinkedIn Outlook Social Connector

This is what I have been using for the last 12 months when working with my Fortune 100 clients' teams. I review this cool tool at least once a week to keep in touch with those people who are in my network and I am looking to keep up-to-date with when I meet with them in offline networking.

I have also recently realized that LinkedIn for Mobiles gives me some of the functionality that the Web version of LinkedIn.com was missing. Namely the activity updates from my LinkedIn members. I use the android version and I can go click on a member's profile and see the recent updates they have written about.

For some reason the mobile team and web team are not connected ☺. Meaning: They develop their code and feature updates separately. So you will see different features enabled on the mobile app that have been disabled on the Web version. Network status updates are one of those features. It is currently enabled on LinkedIn Android App. Check-out this page if you don't already use the

Android version. Go here: https://www.linkedin.com/mobile

Of course I digress here, but back to LinkedIn Outlook Social Connector. What I find amazing, is that this little gem is not written about much. Even Microsoft have not written about it that much on their website properties. Could there be a secret in this?

Here you see a nice "Business Card" view of all your LinkedIn Contacts. Sorted by Last Name. This is very powerful - you cannot do this with LinkedIn Contacts.

I am not going to go into all the details but here are some of the cool features I use when in **Microsoft Outlook**. For your later review, according to Microsoft Outlook - http://bit.ly/16xmuiG

There is also a very nice window pane that Microsoft Outlook Social Connector displays. It displays individual network status updates - a very cool addition to your crm. toolkit.

"The Outlook Social Connector shows updates and information for your contacts in the People Pane, which sits below your open Outlook items, such as e-mail, appointments or meetings, and contacts." Quoted from office.microsoft.com. Download a copy of it from here: http://www.linkedin.com/static?key=microsoft_outlook

Pros

I use it because:

1) I can stay in Microsoft Outlook

2) I can get my updates from my LinkedIn Contacts without leaving Microsoft Outlook Email

3) When LinkedIn Members have turned off their updates (usually by accident) the Social Connector still presents them to you

4) Saves me time having to login to LinkedIn.com and then click on the profile to see the LinkedIn Members updates

5) You can sort and select LinkedIn Members by last name - this is a problem when using contacts.linkedin.com

Cons

1) Requires you to install the app - http://linkd.in/155nXtz and that may slow your system down if you using Microsoft Windows (Windows 7/8) etc.

2) Takes up disk space on your local HDD - every single LinkedIn Member requires a business card view - see screenshot of those updates on the next page

3) Sometimes the Microsoft Outlook Social Connector does not synchronize your LinkedIn Contacts on a timely basis. You may find that recently added contacts do not appear in Outlook

4) Occasionally you may be prompted to add your user name and password details again

LinkedIn Status Updates (via Outlook Connector)

⌂ All Items	Hee- Anonymous	The only job where you start at the top, is digging a hole. –	12:42 PM 9/27/2013
▤ Activities	Hee-.	A little knowledge that acts is worth infinitely more than much knowledge that is idle. – John Quincy Adams	8:42 AM 9/26/2013
✉ Mail	Hee-.	A big shot is a little shot that kept shooting. – Anonymous	8:16 AM 9/20/2013
🔗 Attachments	Hee'	"The measure of success is not whether you have a tough problem to deal with, but whether it is the same problem you had last year." - John...	12:02 PM 9/19/2013
▦ Meetings			
🗩 Status Updates	Hee-'··· – Darrell Royal	Luck is what happens when preparation meets opportunity.	8:26 AM 9/19/2013
	Hee- Winters	If your ship doesn't come in, swim out to it. – Jonathan	8:11 AM 9/12/2013

You see all your LinkedIn Member updates without having to login to LinkedIn.com. Also even if the LinkedIn Member turns this off on their profile you will get the updates.

Here are all my **LinkedIn Social Connector Bookmarks** for you to review.

Ultimate "Cheat Sheet" on Super Connecting - http://linkd.in/1ueb1wI

How to disable the People Pane in Outlook 2010 - http://bit.ly/1naWWft

Frequently asked questions about Outlook Social Connector - http://bit.ly/1n60F07

Outlook 2013 LinkedIn Social Connector – from Supertekboy http://bit.ly/1iRP7Lo

How to Use Social Connector in Microsoft Outlook 2010 - http://bit.ly/MdJIAj

Outlook Social Connector via Zack Whittaker - http://bit.ly/1gItgnF

How to install the Outlook Social Connector (Video) - http://bit.ly/1oUhpqf

Video: Getting the most out of the Outlook Social Connector - http://bit.ly/1gj6RLj

Add LinkedIn to Microsoft Outlook by LinkedIn - http://bit.ly/1kcJMwy

Continued from the previous page.

Turn on the Outlook Social Connector (applies to Outlook 2013) - http://bit.ly/16xmuiG

Office 2013 Tips: Outlook Social Connector – LinkedIn | SCSU IT Guy - http://bit.ly/1iLJ6ut

Go get a copy of LinkedIn Outlook Social Connector today here - http://www.linkedin.com/static?key=microsoft_outlook

BONUS SECTION

Backup your LinkedIn Profile Today!

You have no doubt worked hard to get your LinkedIn Profile looking good and selling your brand/image.

What would you do if for some unknown reason your profile got messed up, or you wanted to go back to a previous LinkedIn profile?

Guess what LinkedIn allows you to recover previous profiles, but the responsibility is all yours! You must do this yourself. Do this at least once a month.

Here are the steps.

Step 1. Go to the Home Menu, then click on Profile

Step 2. Click on the down arrow next to the Edit button

Step 3. Click on Export to PDF

Step 4. Save the PDF on your hard drive

That was easy – wasn't it!!?

Backup your LinkedIn Connections

You need to keep your connections saved offline. After all – didn't it take a long time to accrue the 30,000 connections that you have, or the 500+ whatever the number you have? Here are easy instructions how to do this.

Steps to *Export your LinkedIn connections.

1. Go to the **LinkedIn Toolbar Menu**
2. Click on **Network**
3. Click on **Contacts** under **Network**
4. Click on Settings on the right
5. Under Advanced Settings, click on the Icon that says, **Export LinkedIn Connections**
6. Click on Export (you might get a prompt to enter a *Captcha* word)

Finally you will then get prompted for the output file format. The default is CSV which you can open with **Microsoft Excel™**.

*The above steps work specifically for when you have LinkedIn Contacts enabled. If you have the old menu, just click on **My connections** and then click on the **Export connections.**

How to Ensure your Keywords are Ranking High on Google? (Game Changer I)

This is the new software that not only predicts the keywords that will sell your **LinkedIn Brand,** but will also tell you real time what people will search for. Connect with me on LinkedIn and mention the words **Game Changer I** in the **Subject line** of your message.

Oh and did I mention that it lists all of the keywords potential Amazon Readers are searching for too?

There is a link at the end of this book for you to click. Or you can click here now: http://linkd.in/PLLBUf

How to Connect with Super Connectors on LinkedIn (Even if they are a 3rd Level connection)

The best way to do this is to join the <u>same group</u> as the LinkedIn member belongs to. Most **Super connectors** will have a public profile listing some of the groups they are a member of. Join the same group and then send them a connection request after using advanced search with their name. <u>Don't forget</u> to tell the **LinkedIn Member** why you want to connect! Refer back to <u>page 53</u> for an idea on drafting that message.

Try to join the groups that don't require **moderator approvals**, as you want to join the group instantly and not have to wait for a moderator to respond.

More information on this can be found here: http://bit.ly/10qcT7W

LinkedIn Contacts – the new CRM tool (Game Changer II)

This is absolutely awesome. I can't think of a better way to keep in touch with your hundreds and thousands of connections on LinkedIn. I use this almost every day.

Add to that is the **LinkedIn Outlook Social Connector** - http://linkd.in/155nXtz which I mentioned in the previous chapter.

LinkedIn Contacts is **your virtual online assistant.** There are some downsides, but they are few and far between compared to the added benefits. I love the features such as:

1. Seeing when you first connected with the **LinkedIn Member** you are viewing

2. You can set a **calendar alarm** to connect with one of your existing connections

3. You can add a note to the **LinkedIn connection** you are viewing

Go here for more information: http://contacts.linkedin.com Keep in mind - once you have **LinkedIn Contacts,** you lose the old feature of My LinkedIn Connections and the other menu items associated with it. Also here is an **excellent independent review** of the new contacts tool.

Go here: http://bit.ly/11kYo2m to find out more. You may have to wait awhile before LinkedIn.com will announce to you that you have now been upgraded to the new LinkedIn Contacts.

LinkedIn Updates

I admit it - in this book the I have referred to LinkedIn Signal quite a lot. Unfortunately the LinkedIn.com team decided to remove that app as I previously mentioned. As a result I use the following links mostly for quickly reviewing what my LinkedIn Network Connections have been doing.

LinkedIn Updates Screenshot

http://bit.ly/LinkedIn_Signal - has several subscription options includes information review on: **Salesloft.com**, **Nimble.com Triggerfox.com**.

My personal favorite is to use linkedin.com/updates as you can see on the previous page it keeps you on LinkedIn.com property as well as the ability to categorize the updates by: **Category View**; **Connection View** and **Your Updates**. In the screenshot example I selected the tab, "**Your Updates**."

LinkedIn Skills

Skills on LinkedIn are like stock! Use them wisely and you will see your stock (LinkedIn Brand) rise to the top very quickly. Use skills.linkedin.com to find out what skills are trending down or up on any given day or minute. Try it today at: http://linkedin.com/skills

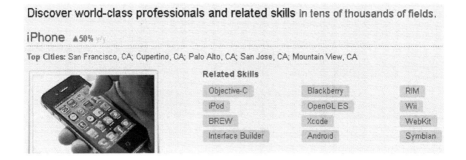

As you can see the iPhone Skill has gone up. It shows it as 50%. The screenshot also indicates some other related skills you can sprinkle in your profile, if you have those skills etc.

Product Development ▼ -3% y/y

Primary Industry: Consumer Goods

In business and engineering, new product development (NPD) is the complete process of bringing a new product to market. A product is a set of benefits offered for exchange and can be tangible (that is, something physical you can touch) or intangible (like a service, experience, or belief). There are two parallel paths involved in the NPD process: one involves the idea generation,...

More on 'Product Development' at Wikipedia »

✓ Listed on your profile   [Edit Your Skills]

If you search for a skill, in this case Product Development, the search will show you if the skill is on your profile already and if it has gone down, or gone up etc. It's a pretty neat LinkedIn tool - hey?

LinkedIn Endorsements

Essentially this LinkedIn endorsement feature is a waste of your precious time. If you are serious about time management you need to turn this feature off - immediately. It adds no real value to your LinkedIn profile. This is just a competing feature of your time, similar to Facebook features.

It's nothing less, nothing more than that. It creates a lot of buzz for the LinkedIn Team, but there is not much sense in using it for smart knowledgeable people, like YOU!

How do you turn this feature off? Check out Erika's viewpoint on her blog. Go here: http://bit.ly/endorse_linkedin Let me forewarn you though - there is a lot of her content that has language which you may find offensive. Be warned!

Now you might have second thoughts and that would be

warranted. **I turned off LinkedIn Endorsements for 6 weeks** and saw my Views and Network search statistics go down by 10%. Also I now use the *Endorsement feature* in conjunction with my **Connecting to Super Connectors** strategy. So I will leave it up to you.

Remember that **LinkedIn Endorsements** are all about your skillset and talent – so be sure to ask your network to endorse you for the skills that are most important to you. Here is my top ten list:

1. New Product Development
2. New Product Introduction
3. Manufacturing Operations Management
4. Stage Gates
5. Phase Gates
6. Publishing
7. Social Media
8. Program Management
9. Process Improvement
10. LinkedIn

To click and endorse my LinkedIn Skill:
http://linkd.in/PLLBUf

More Information on LinkedIn Skill Endorsements:
http://linkd.in/1eoBdfd

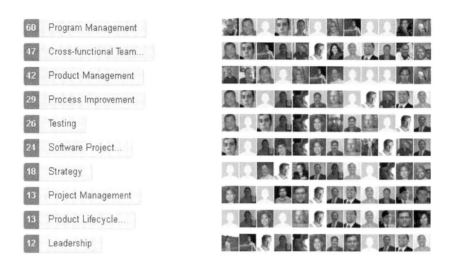

60	Program Management
47	Cross-functional Team...
42	Product Management
29	Process Improvement
26	Testing
24	Software Project...
18	Strategy
13	Project Management
13	Product Lifecycle...
12	Leadership

How do you Endorse the skills that you want to, instead of the ones that LinkedIn prompts you to?

1. Search for the person you want to endorse (type in their name)

2. Click on their profile
3. Scroll down to their Skills & Expertise section (may be in a different place for some LinkedIn Members)
4. Click on the "plus" symbol, as above

Note: If the plus sign is blue, that means you have already endorsed that skill for the **LinkedIn Member**. Shaded Grey are the skills you can endorse and your LinkedIn Connection will love that!

LinkedIn Publisher

After LinkedIn Influencers was introduced on LinkedIn.com, another change came along. This is probably the single best change LinkedIn has made in recent times. Now every LinkedIn member can sell their brand via their LinkedIn profile.

Here is what you need to know about LinkedIn Publisher.

What is LinkedIn Publisher?

The **LinkedIn Publisher** platform allows the member to post full-length content (e.g. blogs/articles) instead of the previous way of using network updates.

LinkedIn Publisher is a great free way to get your message out and establish your brand on a business social media website. It can ensure you are sought after as a thought leader on b2b platform share with world leaders.

It's also known as Long form Posts on LinkedIn. To quote LinkedIn, "While publishing a Long-form post on LinkedIn doesn't mean you're a **LinkedIn Influencer**, publishing allows you to further establish your professional identity by expressing your opinions and sharing your experiences."

For more information type this link into your browser: http://linkd.in/1wh6U7E

Why I recommend you should use LinkedIn Publisher

There are many reasons, here are most of the important ones.

1) Establishes your personal brand

2) Publisher posts can end up going viral and appear in "LinkedIn Pulse"

3) If your employer has a Social Media team you can help grow your company's brand too

4) Keep your published content to around 300-600 words

5) Sprinkle some links throughout the post

6) Post on Thursdays, or Sundays – see http://okdork.com/2014/09/09/linkedin-publishing-success/

7) Once you have published content on LinkedIn.com, share it with other social networks. For example Twitter and Facebook

When not to use LinkedIn Publisher

Are there any times I should not use LinkedIn Publisher? Yes! And Yes! See my earlier point about Thursdays and Sundays being the best days of the week to post.

Don't use **LinkedIn Publisher** to post job opportunities. LinkedIn might revoke your access to this feature.

Posting at certain times and days of the week increases your opportunity to get PVs (Page views/Publisher views).

Don't use LinkedIn Publisher in lieu of Network status. Meaning if you want to post a short network status, like: I have just published a book on, Amazon Secrets Revealed…" use **Network status** and not LinkedIn Publisher.

Tips on using LinkedIn Publisher

Write in an authentic way. Write in a way that starts a conversation with your audience. A conversation will mean that your audience will want to leave comments and interact with you and your post.

Use approved rights approved images. LinkedIn Members are more likely to click on your post with the header photo included to entice your audience to view your content. Remember the old saying, "A picture speaks a thousand words…" or words to that effect.

Give credit to artists and content that you have approval for and use.

Don't use images from Google Images. Procure your image content from recognized sources and have rights to copy. For example you can get images from Flickr.

Try not to use acronyms, or jargon. Keep it simple for your readers to understand.

Start your content with a catchy assertive title. Answer a question. For example, "Why people Lie…" Link: http://linkd.in/1E5FG5X

Here is how you can get started today...

It's as simple as:

- Selecting the Pencil Icon on your LinkedIn Home page

- Writing the post using the LinkedIn Publisher template provided

- Previewing and publishing the post

Further Information on LinkedIn Publisher

More information on LinkedIn Publisher "Best Practices" can be found on LinkedIn.com here: http://linkd.in/1FPMBkv

WITH A STRONG PERSONAL BRAND ON LINKEDIN YOU WILL ACHIEVE SO MUCH MORE

- A strong brand, linked with your resume will get you more calls – guaranteed
- That will then lead to more interview requests
- You can fill in any gaps in your resume with your LinkedIn Profile
- That means **YOU GET HIRED FASTER!**

These days the average job search takes 10 months! Optimize your LinkedIn Profile today before you really need your next job!

In a recent Webinar hosted by **Greig Wells (short link: http://linkd.in/PO5iL8)** he explained a great rule of thumb for figuring out how long it will take you to get hired based on your **LinkedIn Profile Views (who viewed my profile).** Short Link: http://linkd.in/1dksgFZ. Guess what - it's surprisingly simple to use and apply in your future and current job search.

Here it is:

- An average job seeker will take 10 months to find their next job
- A job offer will take around 300 views on LinkedIn
- Therefore if you divide 300 by your views per month (0-2 views by day) and you get 1 view per day it will take you 300/30 = 10 (months)

ABOUT THE AUTHOR

Patrick Gallagher provides his talent & services to a major Fortune 500 company and has spent hours and hours researching about LinkedIn. Patrick has studied many books, tested changes on the LinkedIn.com platform, and has enrolled in many hours of LinkedIn Training.

He enjoys both online and offline networking with professional people from all career professions.

Patrick joined the LinkedIn Professional community platform in 2007 and obtained his **Certified Social Media Professional Certification in 2010**.

Patrick is active in community affairs and regularly volunteers for local charities in the USA. He is originally from the United Kingdom and is married.

He has three children. He currently lives and works in hot, Sunny, Texas.

Patrick is reachable via his **LinkedIn Profile**. A Link is below.
http://linkd.in/PLLBUf:

You can also follow me at my **Twitter page**:
http://bit.ly/Odcjqa.

OTHER BOOKS BY PATRICK X. GALLAGHER

Publishing a Book on Amazon: 7 Steps to Publishing your #1 Book on Amazon Kindle in Minutes!

http://amzn.to/18i9JI3 (USA Link)

http://amzn.to/1bWNnO7 (UK Link)

Kindle Version

Love or Hate Email...21 Rules to Change Your - I Must Check my Email Habit. Get Back to Work and Make Money Again!

http://bit.ly/Love_Email (USA Link)

http://amzn.to/WYox9i (UK Link)

Kindle Version

LinkedIn Secrets Reveal: 10 Secrets to Unlocking Your Complete Profile on LinkedIn.com!

http://amzn.to/12pyCNu (USA Link)

http://amzn.to/162uYqH (UK Link)

Kindle Version

SOURCES – FURTHER READING AND REFERENCE BOOKS

Some of these sources are books that I have read and some are websites that I recommend reviewing for further information. I have included links to my online Amazon Book Library

"How to Write a KILLER LinkedIn Profile...," http://bit.ly/W6dchW by Brenda Bernstein.

"The Power Formula for LinkedIn Success (Second Edition..)," http://amzn.to/10rXzYx by Wayne Breitbarth, 2013.

"LinkedIn Makeover: Professional Secrets to a POWERFUL LinkedIn Profile," http://bit.ly/PMpBZm by Donna Serdula.

"How to REALLY use LinkedIn (Second Edition - Entirely Revised): Discover the true power of LinkedIn and how to leverage it for your business and career," http://amzn.to/Z7o849 by Jan Vermeiren & Bert Verdonck.

"I'm on LinkedIn--Now What??? (Third Edition)," http://amzn.to/1akrAdK by Jason Alba.

Linked Signal - Learn to Extract the "Signal" from the "Noise" online | LinkedIn: http://linkd.in/Qigo8m

How to Really Use LinkedIn with Dive In Deep Training: http://bit.ly/QZKUpZ

LinkedIn Influence 2.0: http://bit.ly/Zj0KQw

Linked InTo Action: http://bit.ly/TxsAEm

LinkedIn Endorsements: http://bit.ly/endorse_linkedin

RECOMMENDED WEBSITES FOR FURTHER REVIEW

Web: **The History of LinkedIn** – http://en.wikipedia.org/wiki/LinkedIn

Web: **About LinkedIn** – http://press.linkedin.com/about

Web: Want-to-stand-out-in-a-job-search-upload-a-photo!: http://nbcnews.to/11l3HP8

Web: http://marketing.linkedin.com/audience

Web: % of Super Connectors: http://bit.ly/11eu9NT

Web: http://linkedintobusiness.com/my-blog/

Web: http://blog.linkedin.com/

Web: LinkedInSecrets on Twitter: http://bit.ly/Odcjqa

Web: LinkedIn User Agreement: http://linkd.in/17MgUYI

Web: How to Use the LinkedIn Contacts Feature: http://bit.ly/11kYo2m

What LinkedIn Books do I recommend to You?

Thanks again for choosing to buy and read my book. I appreciate you have a choice.

Here is my **Top 6 list for LinkedIn Books**. Most of these books are all about completing your profile, unlike mine which documents what you need to do after being 100% complete. The list is <u>not</u> in any order of importance.

1. **LinkedIn Profiles That Don't Suck!** Learn the insider LinkedIn success tactics that will have recruiters calling you! (inspired by Brenda Bernstein, Wayne Breitbarth) - Short Link: http://amzn.to/1ezi7C9

2. **LinkedIn Makeover: Professional Secrets to a POWERFUL LinkedIn Profile** – Short Link: http://amzn.to/1fvWw2D

3. **How to Write a KILLER LinkedIn Profile... And 18 Mistakes to Avoid** – Short Link: http://amzn.to/13Be6u0

4. **I'm on LinkedIn--Now What??? (Third Edition): A Guide to Getting the Most Out of LinkedIn** – Short Link: http://amzn.to/1akrAdK

5. **LinkedIn Marketing: An Hour a Day** – Short Link: http://amzn.to/194t403

6. **Maximum Success with LinkedIn: Dominate Your Market, Build a Global Brand, and Create the Career of Your Dreams** – Short Link: http://amzn.to/1bhJ9Ba

For a more complete list of LinkedIn Books I encourage you to review my Amazon ListMania list: http://amzn.to/17q9isD

There are now over 50 books on the topic of LinkedIn!

By the way **Brenda Bernstein** mentions me in her 8th Edition version of her bestselling book, "**How to Write a KILLER LinkedIn Profile... And 18 Mistakes to Avoid**" – Short Link: http://amzn.to/13Be6u0

Help me to Stamp out LinkedIn Email Phishing!

Always check on **LinkedIn.com** or your **LinkedIn Mobile App** for the same connection request you get sent to your email address. If it is missing on LinkedIn.com you should know it's a disguised way of obtaining your login credentials as the link for connecting in the email is fake.

Be careful when accepting connection requests from people you do not know!

Please check out my Amazon Author page and click the Like Button!

http://www.amazon.com/author/patrickxgallagher

Watch the LinkedIn Book Trailer while you there!

THIS E-BOOK WILL TEACH YOU HOW TO CREATE A COMPETITIVE LINKEDIN FOR BUSINESS PROFILE.

Short Link to YouTube Video: http://bit.ly/16YXr8h

Questions or Comments?

Well done for getting this far and reading this book! Now that you have read the book and put it to good use, I would love to hear from you.

Connect with me via LinkedIn.com.

View my profile on LinkedIn: http://linkd.in/PLLBUf

If you believe this book has helped you and is worth sharing with other potential Amazon Kindle readers, please **leave a review** by **clicking on the button** below.

Get a Rocking LinkedIn Profile Today!

[Create your own review]

Review Link: http://amzn.to/TaxohK

Follow me on **#LinkedIn** -
http://twitter.com/LinkedInSecrets

LinkedInSecrets
@LinkedInSecrets

@TheEssayExpert have you used #LinkedIn
Find References? - pretty cool tool when you
get generic connection requests
pic.twitter.com/ypm3xpZNHt

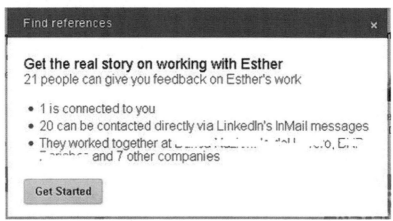

Do you Need to ask me a question and get an instant response? Email me @ **LinkedInSecretsRevealed@gmail.com**

I read and answer all emails sent to me, myself! I do not outsource, or crowd source this task!

Would you like to be featured in my next "*LinkedIn Secrets Revealed Book?*" It's a great way to attract network views to your LinkedIn Profile. Send me an email and I will be sure to add your name and update. Your information may be included in my next e-book update.

You can even add it as a project on your LinkedIn profile! How cool is that?

Cost: It's FREE! Send me an email to the above email address.

Congratulations! By reading and implementing all of these *"LinkedIn Secrets"* you are well on your way to being found faster on **LinkedIn.com** and having even greater success.

While you are asleep there will be people, or companies looking for your products and services - YOU!

You may remind yourself you saved an additional $500 or £500, or €500 by not hiring someone to do it for you!

Easter Egg Fun

Let's pretend it's Easter!

If you bought this book at a **Half Price Books Store** in Austin, Cedar Park, or Round Rock, Texas I will personally send you a kindle copy of two other titles I have published.

Just email me a copy of your receipt with **Subject: Easter Egg**. That's all I need.

Check-out Half Price Books Stores here: http://www.hpb.com/

Email me your receipt @ LinkedInSecretsRevealed@gmail.com

7775050R00065

Printed in Germany
by Amazon Distribution
GmbH, Leipzig